Changing to Survive: Bird Adaptations

by Lillian Duggan

PEARSON

Scott
Foresman

Editorial Offices: Glenview, Illinois • Parsippany, New Jersey • New York, New York
Sales Offices: Needham, Massachusetts • Duluth, Georgia • Glenview, Illinois
Coppell, Texas • Ontario, California • Mesa, Arizona

ISBN: 0-328-13554-2

11 12 13 14 15 16 V054 15 14 13 12 11 10

Birds Everywhere

They soar above the clouds like graceful airplanes. Birds can be found nearly everywhere on Earth— from land to sea, desert to tropical rain forest. They are beautiful and diverse. They live all over the world, even ice-covered Antarctica. Some birds spend their lives on the open ocean and move onto land only to nest. Other birds never leave the ground.

There are many kinds of habitats in the world. Some places are hot and dry, while others are cold and wet. Each habitat has challenges for its animal life to overcome. In order to survive in a habitat, an animal must be able to adapt, or change. These changes **enable,** or make it possible for, an animal to survive in its home.

Birds are one of the most successful animals on Earth. They have adapted to so many different places that they inhabit every type of habitat in the world!

In this book, you'll see how each bird has adapted to survive in its home.

The black-throated sparrow is adapted to life in the desert. It can go without drinking water for days.

3

From the First Bird to Flying Machines

The first birds were probably relatives of prehistoric reptiles. Scientists have animal fossils with wings and feathers from 150 million years ago. These animals also had reptile features, such as teeth, claws, and a long tail. Scientists named this ancient animal *Archaeopteryx.* The wings and feathers of Archaeopteryx show that it could fly, but scientists don't think it stayed in the air for a very long time.

Over thousands of years, birds have evolved into flying machines. Their bodies are well suited for air travel. Birds are faster and can stay in the air longer than other flying animals, such as bats or insects. Certain birds have been known to fly 100 miles per hour and travel over a thousand miles without stopping.

How do birds do this? It helps that birds have wings and bodies that are almost completely covered with feathers.

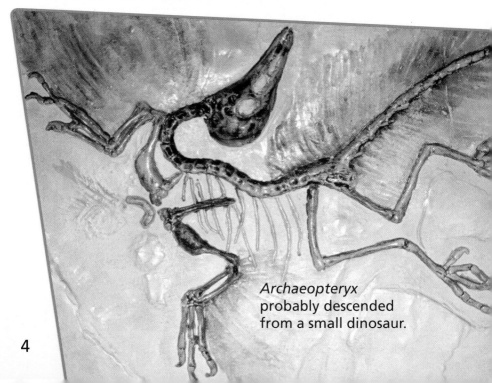

Archaeopteryx probably descended from a small dinosaur.

Hollow bones enable a bird to use less energy during flight.

A bird's beak appears thick and heavy, but it is made of lightweight, though hard, material.

Flying takes a lot of energy. For birds to be such great fliers, they must save as much energy as they can. They can save energy because their bodies are so light. Their bones are thin, and some are even hollow. Even a bird's beak is thin and lightweight.

To get the energy they need to fly, birds eat a lot. For small creatures, they have big appetites. In fact, birds eat more food than other animals the same size. They also choose foods high in energy, such as seeds, fruits, fish, worms, and insects. Birds digest food quickly so they can use the energy right away.

Homes Around the World

Birds live in nearly every corner of Earth. Each new location had its own set of challenges that birds have had to adapt to in order to survive. Some birds have long beaks; others have short ones. Some have long legs while others need short legs. Some birds fly fast, while others never leave the ground.

In this book, you will read about eight different groups of birds, including—

Sea Birds

Shore Birds

Water Birds

Woodpeckers

Expert Fliers

Land Birds

You'll see how they had to adapt to survive.

Sea Birds

The ocean is probably the hardest place for birds to survive. There is a bird that spends most of its life in the air above the ocean. This bird is called the wandering albatross. It may look pretty tiring to stay airborne so long, but the albatross has adapted to make flying easy. With nearly an eleven-foot wingspan, this bird uses the flow of ocean air to glide effortlessly.

Penguins are seabirds too. Living in the cold region of Antarctica, penguins may not fly, but they're great swimmers and divers. Instead of wings, they use flippers to push themselves through the water. Webbed feet and a tail help them to steer.

Penguins have also adapted to survive in freezing cold ocean water. Thick layers of waterproof feathers keep them warm and dry. Below the feathers, a layer of fat keeps them warm.

Emperor penguins are the only animals that spend the winter on the ice in Antarctica.

The wandering albatross is almost always in flight. It returns to land only to breed.

9

This common snipe is enjoying an underground meal.

Shore Birds

Shore birds spend so much time in shallow water that they're also called wading birds. Shore birds usually have long, pointy beaks and long, thin legs. They like being close to land. Their pointy beaks help them dig in dirt or sand for worms, insects, crabs, and snails. Long legs keep the rest of their bodies dry above water.

Shore birds, such as sandpipers and plovers, live all around the world. Sandpipers live along shorelines and in marshes. They eat snails and worms in the winter and insects in the summer. Sandpipers have mastered the art of catching and swallowing their prey with their bills still underground!

The pheasant-tailed jacana eats invertebrates, frogs, and fish.

Unlike many other shore birds, plovers have shorter beaks and legs. They don't need long beaks because they eat above the water. With their short legs, plovers spend less time in the water than sandpipers.

One plover, the wrybill, has a beak that bends to the right. It looks funny, but it's useful. This shape helps the wrybill easily get food from under stones. The New Zealand wrybill walks in circles while it hunts for food.

Another shore bird, the jacana, is known for its unique feet. The jacana's toes and claws are long and spread out. These special feet enable it to walk on wobbly surfaces like floating lily pads. The jacana lives in lakes, marshes, and ponds in Africa, India, China, and Southeast Asia.

Water Birds

Water birds live near lakes, rivers, ponds, and marshes. These are great nesting spots. They are surrounded by tall plants that keep the birds safe and hidden.

Flamingos may be the most beautiful and unusual water birds. They are large with long legs and necks. The flamingo is perhaps one of the most popular birds in the world. Who can help but admire its long, curvy neck and pretty pink color? Flamingos have an unusual downward-pointing beak. They stick their heads in the water upside-down to find food, using their beaks like scoops. The flamingo's muscular tongue pumps water into its beak. Then, the water is strained out, leaving tiny plants and animals behind.

Geese, ducks, and swans live on ponds and lakes from big cities to the remote tundra. These birds are built for swimming. They have webbed feet, which they use like paddles to push themselves through the water. They not only swim well, but they are good fliers. They migrate great distances each winter to warmer areas in the south.

Mallard ducks are beautiful and colorful. Like other ducks, mallards get food from the water's surface. The sides of their bills are lined with filters that strain food from the water. They are also very resourceful. They are willing to get food in many ways, such as taking scraps from people's hands.

Like the flamingo, the pelican is an unusual-looking water bird. They have the longest bills of any bird. Pelicans use a pouch on their bills to catch fish. When the pelican plunges its bill below the surface of the water, its pouch opens up. The water drains out of the pouch, and then the pelican enjoys its meal. Like ducks, pelicans have webbed feet to help them steer in water. They're also good fliers, and many migrate over long distances. The great white pelican lives in parts of Africa, Europe, and Asia.

Sometimes mallards dive into shallow water to feed from the bottom.

Great white pelicans feed in groups, herding fish together.

Flamingos' feathers turn pink because of pigments in the foods they eat.

Farmers used to rely on barn owls to keep their grain safe from hungry rodents.

Birds of Prey

Birds of prey are hunters. Eagles, hawks, and buzzards are all birds of prey. They have powerful eyesight that allows them to find their prey, or food, easily. They have sharp claws for catching animals and hooked beaks for tearing their food.

Owls are nocturnal, which means they hunt at night. Owls are known for their huge eyes in the front of their faces. They can hunt well in the dark because of their powerful eyes and ears. They can also rotate their heads almost all the way around to search for prey. Unlike most birds, owls have feathers with soft edges, making it easy for them to sneak up on their prey quietly.

Barn owls spend their days resting inside tree holes or barns. They eat mostly mice and other rodents. They can catch these rodents in total darkness because of their powerful hearing.

Pale Male, a City Hawk

The city is a noisy place with a lot of buildings. Red-tailed hawks love open spaces where they can soar in the sky for hours. It seems unusual that they live in cities. In fact, a particular red-tailed hawk lives in one of the largest cities in the world, New York City. Pale Male, is a real New Yorker. Pale Male got his name because his feathers are lighter in color than those of other red-tailed hawks.

Some red-tailed hawks migrate from Canada to Mexico or Central America in the winter, passing through New York City. In 1991, Pale Male decided to stick around in the Big Apple.

Surprisingly, Pale Male has lived in New York ever since. Living near the city's largest park, Central Park, he can easily find food. He can swoop down from his lookout spot and snatch up prey in seconds. He has had several mates and produced many offspring. Pale Male and a recent mate raised their young in a nest on the ledge of an apartment building overlooking Central Park.

Pale Male has lived in New York City since 1991.

15

Songbirds

Some birds are known for making beautiful music. These are called songbirds. Some songbirds simply string a few notes together, while others sing enchanting songs. The songs of the lark and the nightingale are two of the most admired. Songbirds sing to attract mates or to defend their homes. Except for a few species, only males have this talent.

Songbirds are also called perching birds, because they have special feet that help them balance on tree branches. Three of their four toes point forward and one points backward. This enables songbirds, or perching birds, to wrap their toes around a branch or a wire easily.

Songbirds have different types of beaks, depending on what they eat. White-winged crossbills have beaks with crossed tips that **specialize** in eating cone seeds. They use their beaks to pry apart the scales of the cones. Then their tongues lift out the seed hidden between the scales. Crossbills can eat three thousand seeds in a single day!

The white-winged crossbill's unique beak is adapted for eating cone seeds.

Like the nightingale, the mockingbird is a famous singer. The mockingbird can copy the calls of other bird species. It can also mimic the sounds of other animals and objects, such as saws. Mockingbirds use their songs for protection, and their constant singing tells other birds to stay away.

The North American dipper is a songbird that has adapted to life on the water. Its name comes from the habit of quickly raising and lowering their bodies into the water by bending their legs. It lives in mountain streams and ponds. The dipper has strong feet that can grip slippery rocks in the water. It perches on these rocks and dips its head underwater to search for food. Insects, worms, snails, small fish, and fish eggs make up the dipper's diet. When the dipper spots a tasty meal, it either wades into the water or dives under. Dippers aren't good surface swimmers, but they are fast underwater. They even flap their wings in underwater "flight." They have a thick undercoat of feathers, which keeps them warm. They also have flaps that close their nostrils to keep out water and an extra clear eyelid to protect their eyes.

North American dippers build their nests on stream rocks or beneath waterfalls.

Northern mockingbirds spend most of their time running or hopping on the ground.

17

Woodpeckers

You may have heard the tapping of a woodpecker and not known what it was. Woodpeckers eat insects that live in tree trunks and on leaves.

Woodpeckers have a unique way of finding food. With its heavy, pointed beak, a woodpecker hammers into tree bark to find insects. When the woodpecker finds an insect, it stretches out its long, sticky tongue and grabs it. Some woodpeckers have prickles or special **mucus**, or thick sticky fluid, on their tongues for snatching up insects.

Woodpecker

A woodpecker's head has also adapted to protect itself. Woodpeckers peck hard and quickly, like a jackhammer. Their brains need protection from this repetitive jarring motion. Woodpecker's skulls are made up of spongy, shock-absorbing bones.

Land Birds

We usually think of birds as flying animals. Most birds do fly, but there are some that don't. Some land birds have wings that are too small for flying. Some land birds can fly, but they only use their wings to make short flights into the trees at night. These birds are known as game birds. They include turkeys, pheasants, and quails.

Some land birds have become fast runners, with long, strong legs. The fastest of these is the ostrich. The ostrich is the largest and heaviest bird in the world. Ostriches are nearly six feet tall. They weigh between two and three hundred pounds. An ostrich can run forty-three miles per hour, making it able to outrun most of its enemies.

The ostrich is well adapted to its environment. It lives in semi-desert and grassland areas in Africa, where it can walk a long way in search of food. Plant shoots and leaves, flowers, and seeds make up most of its diet.

Ostriches travel in flocks of ten to fifty birds in search of food.

Expert Fliers

Some birds are better fliers than others. Many skilled fliers have interesting ways to get food. Hummingbirds, for example, can beat their wings more than fifty times per second, allowing them to hover in mid-air. A hummingbird uses its long beak to drink nectar from flowers.

The ruby-throated hummingbird lives in forests. It migrates to Central America for the winter, flying nonstop across the Gulf of Mexico.

Many expert fliers catch their food straight out of the air. The European bee-eater specializes in eating bees and wasps. It captures its prey in mid-air. The bee-eater rubs the insect on a branch to destroy its stinger before eating it, and then swallows up the nonstinging insects.

Swifts are fast and skilled. Because they have small legs and feet, swifts don't walk much. These birds can do almost everything in the air. They catch insects, eat, and drink while in flight. Nesting is the only activity swifts must do on land. The Eurasian swift spends two to three years in flight without landing!

Eurasian swifts feed on small airborne insects and spiders.

A ruby-throated hummingbird can beat its wings fifty-three times a second.

The European bee-eater's long, pointed beak helps it grasp large insects.

Bird Conservation

Birds have adapted in many ways to different types of habitats. Unfortunately, growing cities, pollution, and cutting down trees have hurt birds' habitats.

Adaptation takes many years. Many birds have not been able to adapt quickly enough to changes in their habitats. Some of them are now extinct, or no longer exist. Others are still around thanks to the help of conservationists. Conservationists help endangered animals survive.

Sometimes supplies in a bird's habitat become **scarce**, or in short supply. This scarcity happens when a habitat is destroyed. Conservationists help birds by trying to get laws passed that protect their habitat.

When conservationists help animals to breed, they help them to grow. Zoos around the world have breeding programs.

These programs bring birds into the zoo where they can mate and have babies. Breeding is **critical**, or absolutely necessary, when a species is endangered.

Scientists who work with birds have special training. They need to understand how to care for young birds. Baby birds must be kept in a **sterile** place that is free from harmful bacteria in order to keep them healthy.

Conservationists have saved a large number of bird species from extinction.

Glossary

critical *adj.* absolutely necessary.

enable *v.* to make possible.

mucus *n.* a thick liquid that moistens and protects body parts.

scarce *adj.* lacking an amount that is enough to meet demand.

specialize *v.* to put efforts toward a particular activity.

sterile *adj.* free from harmful bacteria.